Along with having my two-year-old son in my arms helping me prepare dinner, I look forward to using this book to further grow our relationship and the knowledge of the culinary classics.

—Henry Garcia
Executive Chef, The Palms Hotel & Casino,
Las Vegas, NV

Published by Tate Publishing & Enterprises, LLC
127 E. Trade Center Terrace | Mustang, Oklahoma 73064 USA
1.888.361.9473 | www.tatepublishing.com

Tate Publishing is committed to excellence in the publishing industry. The company
reflects the philosophy established by the founders, based on Psalm 68:11,
"The Lord gave the word and great was the company of those who published it."

Book design copyright © 2009 by Tate Publishing, LLC. All rights reserved.
Cover and Interior design by Elizabeth A. Mason
Illustrations by Jason Hutton
Conceptual designs by Brenda L. Tuttle

Published in the United States of America

ISBN: 978-1-60799-441-1
1. Juvenile Nonfiction: Cooking & Food
2. Juvenile Nonfiction: General
09.04.15

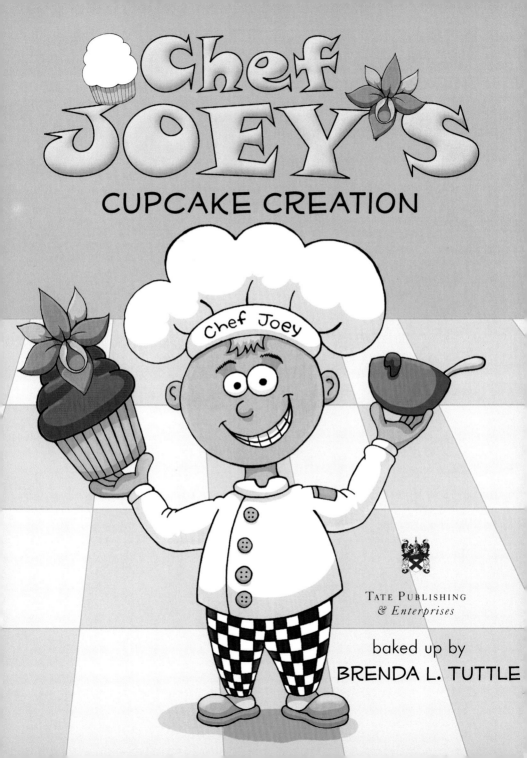

Once upon a time,
an amazing chef was born.
His name was

Joey.

Joey

was creative, curious and had

a busy mind. He created a

CUPCAKE that was one of a kind.

So flip through the pages and

soon you will find how to create

this CUPCAKE in just a short time.

Chef Joey encourages you

to find an adult to help you make

these CUPCAKES too!

Through the grocery store **Chef Joey** traveled with ease, he knew just what he wanted to make his masterpiece. Into his cart he gathered these...

CHOCOLATE CAKE MIX, EGGS, CANOLA OIL, COCOA, UNSALTED BUTTER, MILK, POWDERED SUGAR, CHOCOLATE CHIPS AND VANILLA EXTRACT.

Chef Joey

returned to his kitchen and washed his hands. He placed all his groceries on the counter and chose his

CUPCAKE PANS.

After **Chef Joey** turned on his OVEN to 350°F degrees, he mixed 1 BOX OF CHOCOLATE CAKE MIX, 1–1/3 CUPS WATER, 1/3 CUP CANOLA OIL AND 3 LARGE EGGS for 2 minutes with a mixer on medium speed, to make the raw version of his masterpiece*.

The CUPCAKE PANS were lined with assorted colored paper and a handful of CHOCOLATE CHIPS were added to enhance the cake batter flavor. The CUPCAKES spent about 16 to 20 minutes in the hot, hot oven, as Chef Joey made the rich CHOCOLATE FROSTING to use as the topping.

For the frosting, **Chef Joey** used a mixer on medium speed, as he combined these ingredients... 1 STICK (1/2 CUP) UNSALTED BUTTER, MELTED, 1/4 CUP PEANUT BUTTER (IF DESIRED), 2/3 CUP COCOA POWDER, 3 CUPS POWDERED SUGAR, 1/3 CUP MILK, 1 TEASPOON VANILLA EXTRACT... and they were beaten until the mixture could spread very easily*.

Fresh from the oven, the smell of HOT CUPCAKES filled the air. Chef Joey frosted the cooled, moist CUPCAKES and garnished them by placing a fresh, PURPLE ORCHID on top to add a decorative flare.

Chef Joey

has created a yummy TREAT

for his TUMMY!

HAPPY BAKING,

Chef Joey

Fun Cupcake Facts

- CUPCAKES were named because they are a small cake that is the same size as a TEACUP.

- A long time ago, CUPCAKES were baked in individual pottery cups or RAMEKINS (small bowls).

- People in Britain call cupcakes "FAIRY CAKES."

- HOSTESS CUPCAKES were first made in 1919. In 1950, the squiggly lines were added to the top of the cupcake frosting.

The recipes found in this book are not original creations. They can be found on packaged goods (such as cake mix) in stores where groceries are sold.

listen|imagine|view|experience

AUDIO BOOK DOWNLOAD INCLUDED WITH THIS BOOK!

In your hands you hold a complete digital entertainment package. Besides purchasing the paper version of this book, this book includes a free download of the audio version of this book. Simply use the code listed below when visiting our website. Once downloaded to your computer, you can listen to the book through your computer's speakers, burn it to an audio CD or save the file to your portable music device (such as Apple's popular iPod) and listen on the go!

How to get your free audio book digital download:

1. Visit www.tatepublishing.com and click on the e|LIVE logo on the home page.
2. Enter the following coupon code:
   6247-0f8d-f690-a516-7f07-3a4d-6d99-fee9
3. Download the audio book from your e|LIVE digital locker and begin enjoying your new digital entertainment package today!